PET OWNER'S GUIDE TO THE
BULLDOG

Judith Daws

RINGPRESS

I would like to dedicate this book to my mother, Dora Wakefield, who taught me almost all I know about Bulldogs.

ACKNOWLEDGEMENTS

Thanks to my husband, Brian, for his endless encouragement and to my three sons and their wives (Martin and Sarah, Neil and Sue, and Simon and Kate) for helping me out with my computer problems and proof-reading.

ABOUT THE AUTHOR

Judith Daws has bred many Champions, both here and overseas. Her kennel, Outdoors, is the only one to have won Best Dog and Best Bitch at Bulldog of the Year, the most prestigious event in the Bulldog calendar. Judith is an international Championship judge, and has judged as far afield as Japan. She has also bred, showed and judged Bichon Frise for more than 20 years.

Cover photography: Outdoors Above Turn, bred and owned by Judith Daws. Photo: Julia Barnes
Designed by: Sara Howell

Published by Ringpress Books Limited, PO Box 8, Lydney, Gloucestershire, GL15 4YN, United Kingdom.

First published 2000
©2000 Ringpress Books Limited. All rights reserved

ISBN 1 86054 112 7

Printed and bound in Hong Kong through Printworks International Ltd.

CONTENTS

1 Origins Of The Bulldog

Today's loveable Bulldog is very different from his fighting ancestors. It is hard to imagine that this gentle, happy-go-lucky dog could have once existed to bait bulls. The modern Bulldog bears little resemblance in structure or temperament to the fierce war-dog

The charm of the 'beautifully ugly' Bulldog.

that gave the breed its name.

A symbol of the British spirit, it would be difficult to imagine John Bull without his Bulldog. A companion dog, with great affection for, and faithfulness to, his master, the Bulldog is dignified and distinctive in appearance, and, when you are out walking with him, he will always be admired. He is placid and trustworthy with children, but his stance and sour expression will frighten away intruders. A quiet dog that only barks when there is good reason, the Bulldog is never demanding, and can be lazy, if allowed.

Properly trained, he will enjoy walking and outings in the car. He can be extremely stubborn and slow to obey, but, with time and patience, he can become the perfect pet. Above all, he is unquestionably loyal, has great strength of character and is often said to be 'beautifully ugly'.

HISTORY OF THE BREED

The early origins of the Bulldog breed are somewhat obscure, with most dog historians agreeing to differ. The Bulldog is certainly one of the oldest breeds, and first appeared in literature in 1500, when he was called the 'Bonddogge', 'Boldogge' or 'Bulldogge'. Later in that century, the name 'Bandogge' was mentioned by William Shakespeare in his play *King Henry VI Part II*, and, in 1585, William Harrison described the breed in *Description of England* (1585):

"Because manie of them are tied up in chaines and strong bonds in the daietime for doing hurt abroad, which is a huge dog, stubborn, ouglie, eager, burtenhouse of bodie (and therefore of little swiftness), terrible and fearful to behold, and oftentimes more fierce and fell than anie Archadian or Corsican cur."

Roughly translated, this means that many Bulldogs were bound up with strong chains and bonds to make them more savage when released! Yes, they were bred and trained to fight to kill. Equally, one must realise they had great courage, as they had to bait bears, lions and bulls.

British Bulldogs were popular with bullfighters in Spain. Some early writers say the name of the breed was derived from the shape of the head being similar to that of the bull. Others say the Bulldog took his name from his main function, which was to attack the bull.

Courage and the ability to endure pain led to the exploitation of the breed.

The first modern spelling of the Bulldog was found in a letter written by Prestwick Eaton of San Sebastian, to George Willingham of St Swithin's Lane, London, in 1631. According to A Monograph by Edgar Farman (second edition, 1901), the writer asked for several things to be forwarded to him, including "a good Mastive dogge" and "two good Bulldoggs".

The playwright and poet Ben Jonson also mentions the Bulldog in his play *The Silent Woman* in the early 1600s.

BULL-BAITING

During the Middle Ages, the sport of bull-baiting was extremely popular in England. It was patronised by all classes, from the highest to the lowest in the land, and great amounts of money changed hands in wagers on the outcome of these contests. Almost every town or village in England had its own bull-ring. The animals that were baited were primarily bulls and bears, although monkeys, lions, badgers and other animals were also used. During a bait, the fighting dogs were pitted in a battle to death with another animal for the amusement of the townsfolk.

It was a cruel, barbaric sport, which exploited the Bulldog for many years because of his courage and capacity to endure pain. It was once written that not only was he the most courageous dog, but also the most courageous animal, in the world.

Writing in *British Sportsman, or Nobleman, Gentleman, and Farmer's Dictionary* in 1792, William Augustus Osbaldeston describes the Bulldog as "one of the most fierce and strong of the canine race, having a short nose, and the under jaw larger than the

Early Bulldogs were lighter than present-day dogs.

upper. The breed is in a manner peculiar to England; but ever since the savage custom of bull-baiting has happily been on the decline, it has suffered neglect. Such is the strength and ferocity of these animals, that four of them have been known to master a lion and when they are turned loose on a bull and have properly seized him, nothing short of loss of life or the giving way of the part can disengage them. While that barbarous amusement continued in vogue, various instances of savage fortitude have occurred in the feats of this breed, which would scarcely be credited in countries where the diversions are more rational and elegant."

The early Bulldogs were not so heavily built as they are today. You only have to look at some of the old pictures to see that they were lighter in body and bone, higher on the legs, and had longer tails

The breed is now recognised as the big 'softie' of the canine world.

Once you have fallen for the charms of a Bulldog, no other breed will do.

and smaller heads. They had tremendous stamina, and were powerful and ferocious – certainly not the soft-hearted companions they are today.

THE FIRST BREED CLUBS

In 1835, bull-baiting was made illegal in Britain by Act of Parliament, and Bulldog breeding diminished, as the dogs were no longer in demand. If it had not been for a small group of dedicated fanciers, Bulldogs may have been lost forever. Fortunately, a team of true lovers of the breed, and a former owner of fighting dogs, got together, with the desire to retain the breed and all its good points.

In 1864, the first Bulldog Club was formed with the motto 'Hold Fast'. Unfortunately, the club only lasted three years, but during this time, the first Breed Standard was written. It was called the 'Philo-Kuan' Standard, as Philo Kuan was the nom de plume of the Standard's author, Samuel Wickens.

The Philo-Kuan Standard of the British Bulldog (Canis Pugnax) stated:

"The British Bulldog is a majestic, ancient animal, very scarce, much maligned, and, as a rule, very little understood. If treated with kindness, often noticed and frequently with his master, he is a quiet and tractable dog: but if kept chained up and little noticed, he becomes less sociable and

docile and, if excited and made savage, he is a most dangerous animal. He is generally an excellent guard, an extraordinary water dog and very valuable to cross with Terriers, Hounds, Greyhounds etc., to give them courage and endurance. He is the boldest and most resolute of animals. The Gamecock is a courageous bird, but he will only attack his own species; but there is nothing a good bulldog will not attack, and ever brave and unappalled, with matchless courage, he will give up only with life itself."

In 1875, The Bulldog Club Incorporated was formed. It was the forerunner of all dog clubs in the world, and existed before the UK Kennel Club was conceived. Members drew up a Standard similar to the Philo-Kuan, which is still used today and varies only

The popularity of the breed is evident in the number of Bulldog collectables that are available.

slightly from the official Standard. It is thanks to that small group of determined men, well over 100 years ago, that the breed gradually lost its undesirable characteristics and became the fireside pet it is today.

BULLDOG COLLECTABLES

Bulldog memorabilia is collected by many; even people who have never owned a Bulldog find it interesting.

There are at least six different sets of stamps issued by various countries – Afghanistan in 1988, Albania in 1966, Eritrea in 1984, Laos in 1982, Ras-al-Khaima in 1971 and Nicaragua in 1974.

Postcards depicting the Bulldog are very popular with collectors. Popular themes include the 'beauty and the beast' type of illustration, featuring beautiful girls or innocent children, and the 'advert' variety, used to portray the 'Britishness' of a product. Cigarette cards often featured the Bulldog, some dating back to 1890.

The breed has always been a challenge to the artist. In the early days, there were many paintings and engravings showing the fighting dog. There were numerous oil paintings depicting famous show dogs. In recent times, prints showing the Bulldog and his canine friends playing cards or pool have become popular, especially in British public houses.

Bulldog models are probably the most popular collectors' item. They come in all shapes and sizes and in various materials, from bone china, pottery, bronze, brass, pewter, and even cement for the large outside models. The most valuable ones are the antique limited editions, which can occasionally still be found in antique shops, auctions, or even car-boot sales. I well remember a young couple who came to me to pick up their new puppy. Their journey took less time than expected, so they decided to stop off at a car-boot sale a few miles from my house. On the first stall they approached, they found a beautiful old model, so they went home with two Bulldogs – one much easier to look after than the other! Some models also feature Winston Churchill, who is often associated with the Bulldog, although he never owned one.

I could go on to mention more items featuring Bulldogs that are popular with collectors: posters, plates, china tea sets, doorstops, walking sticks, jewellery – but I'll leave it to you to start looking for yourself.

2 The Bulldog Character

Unfortunately, the poor Bulldog receives more than his fair share of bad press about his character. Even his intelligence is sometimes questioned – but, like all breeds, individuals differ greatly. If properly trained, and treated kindly and firmly, he can hold his own with other breeds. And what about his good points? I can relate a few stories that demonstrate his wonderful temperament, unchanged for many years.

FAITHFULNESS

Back in the 1860s, 'Old King Dick' was a universal favourite. He belonged to Jacob Lamphier, a well-known breeder. During the last year of his life, Jacob was afflicted with consumption and was often confined to his bed, with Dick as his constant companion. When Jacob died, and until after his funeral, Dick was confined to the yard. On the first day he was let loose, he instantly rushed upstairs, into his master's room, and made straight for the chair Jacob used to sit in. He put his paws on the bed, then looked under it, and he ran back and forth, crying piteously. Miss Lamphier tried to comfort him, without success. He lay down on the mat and never seemed to lift his head again. He refused all food, and although every effort was made to stimulate him, he died four days later.

Another tale, from H Webb's *Dogs* (1872), and signed 'JB':

"Many years ago, I was walking through Chapel St, when I was attracted by the conduct of two dogs, the one a bulldog, the other a sort of mastiff, much larger and evidently longing for battle. He attacked and tried to make him fight, but the bulldog, whose very countenance expressed good temper, after defending himself at first, quietly walked away.

The Bulldog does not deserve the bad press he sometimes receives.

Determined to quarrel with somebody, the mastiff seized a small terrier, and laid him shrieking and yelping on his back, in an instant the generous bulldog flew back to the rescue and drove off the savage and walked away. The mastiff watched the retreating hero, and when he thought he was far enough away, he attacked the poor little victim for a second time, but the champion heard his cry and again rushed to his aid. This time the bulldog did not leave him. The terrier rubbed his nose against his friend's and wagged his tail and whispered in his ear that he still needed protection. They walked away together, the bulldog evidently would see him safely home. The tyrant did not venture to attack him again, but stood looking subdued and sulky. Several persons with myself were spectators of the canine generosity and ill-temper."

STUBBORNNESS
A characteristic of the Bulldog that fascinates many people is his stubbornness. He is certainly not a

dog who will jump at your every command; he will obey, but only when he is ready. If he decides he does not want to go for a walk or get out of your car, you have a weighty problem on your hands!

Some years ago, my parents bred a beautiful puppy, Jubilant, for whom they had high hopes in the show ring. However, Jubilant had other ideas, and refused to walk away from the house or the kennels. He was fine in the garden; he walked and stood for show like a dream, but if he was taken through the gate, he would sit solid as a rock, and all attempts to encourage and coax him were ignored. It was a few weeks before his first show, and, in desperation,

Faithful, kindly and stubborn – the hallmarks of the breed.

The Bulldog is renowned for his stubborn streak.

my father decided on a new approach. He put Jubi in his wheelbarrow and pushed him all the way into the village. He left the barrow at a friend's house, lifted Jubi out and said "come on, we are going home". To his relief and amazement, the puppy trotted by his side all the way home. This episode had to be repeated several times before he eventually managed to persuade him to walk away from the house, as well as back to it. His first show was nerve-racking, but he behaved impeccably and really showed off as he walked; you could almost hear him saying, "I can do it when I want to". He won best

puppy and went on to become a Champion at a very young age.

PROTECTIVENESS

Bulldogs are certainly not a vicious breed, but they do show great courage in protecting their owners and family. Their appearance can be a deterrent to any would-be intruders; most visitors will stand at the gate, look at the dog, and ask if it is safe to come in. If you then invite them to enter and they act in an amiable way towards your Bulldog, they will have made a friend for life.

One of my fellow breeders was very grateful when one of his

If properly supervised, Bulldogs get on well with children.

bitches showed her teeth! He was sleeping on the kitchen floor by the side of his bitch, Bella, and her new litter of puppies. Bella was unusually restless and began to bark. She was told to be quiet, but she paced the floor, growled, and persisted in barking at the door. Realising that he was not going to be allowed to sleep, my friend started to rouse himself. By now, Bella was barking frantically; the door opened and a terrified intruder took one look at Bella and ran out of the house, leaving everything he had strategically placed by the door for a quick getaway. Needless to say, the family is very proud of its wonderful pet, perfect mother and ferocious security guard.

DEVOTION

The Bulldog's devotion to his loved ones is a joy, but it can also be exasperating. He always wants to be near you, to sit right in front of your fire, snoring his head off so you can hardly hear the TV. He will lie right in the doorway, appearing completely unmoved when you almost trip over him.

The Bulldog is a well-known face throughout the world.

If you should accidentally tread on him, he will seldom flinch, but he may lift his head with a look of disgust.

The Bulldog is excellent with children. He will tolerate poking and prodding without becoming annoyed. Of course, children must never be left unsupervised with any dog, and should be taught to have respect for their pet and to know that there are times when he needs peace and quiet. He may do things that make you angry, but he will never be angry with you – he will just give you a woebegone look if he thinks he has been the cause of offence.

THE MAIN ATTRACTION
The Bulldog enjoys being the centre of attention and is therefore a popular model. He has played several film, TV and theatre roles, and it is said that he is the most photographed dog in the world. He has been used extensively in advertising, and is often used as a mascot for sports teams and the armed forces. Violinist Nigel Kennedy will only appear on stage if arrangements are made to accommodate his pet Bulldog!

3 Choosing a Bulldog

Before buying any breed of puppy, there are various questions to consider.

1. Can you make a lifelong commitment to a dog? The Bulldog's average lifespan is ten years.
2. Can you afford to feed him properly and to pay his veterinary fees?
3. Is your house big enough and do you have an adequate garden?
4. Are you prepared to exercise him every day, whatever the weather?
5. Is there someone at home for most of the day to care for the puppy's needs?
6. Are you sure this is the breed that *you* want? Do not buy a puppy just because your children want one. They will very quickly grow up and find other interests, or leave home, and you will be left to care for the dog.

The charms of a Bulldog puppy are hard to resist, but think hard before you take on a lifelong commitment.

Make absolutely sure the breeder is selling purebred Bulldogs.

If you can answer 'yes' to all these questions, the next step is to start looking for your chosen breed. Be prepared to take your time, to think about your preferences and to have a good look around before making a decision. You would not buy that first car you saw, or the first coat! Remember, all puppies are adorable at six to eight weeks old; you must see the adults, and be sure they also appeal to you and that they will fit in with your lifestyle.

LOCATING PUPPIES

The correct name of the breed is simply Bulldog, not 'English Bulldog' or 'British Bulldog'.

You must take care to ensure that you are buying a purebred Bulldog. Unfortunately, there are people breeding and selling puppies which they call 'Olde English Bulldogs', 'Regency Bulldogs' and 'American Bulldogs', to name but a few. These are crossbred dogs and are not pedigree Bulldogs.

Your national Kennel Club can give you details of Bulldog Clubs, and if you contact your nearest, the secretary will be able to recommend local breeders to you.

Any reputable breeder should be happy to allow you to visit their kennel, even if they do not have puppies available, to discuss the breed and their needs.

However, if you make an appointment to visit, please be sure to keep it, or to telephone if you are not able to keep the appointment. Breeders have a very busy routine, and it is annoying to have rushed around preparing for visitors who do not turn up.

Avoid breeders who tell you that their puppies are guaranteed to become show winners. No one can predict how a puppy will end up. Some do not make the necessary size; some grow too big; ears may not settle correctly, and, with the second teeth, they can go wry-jawed. So much will depend on how the puppy is fed, exercised and trained. I have seen several puppies that showed great potential at eight weeks, but, at six months, although they were strong, healthy dogs, they certainly were not going to become Champions!

MEETING THE PUPPIES

Most breeders do not like you to view the puppies until they are five to six weeks old. It is not fair for the mother to be disturbed; she needs peace and quiet to rear her babies. By six weeks of age, the puppies are running around and developing their characters, but do not touch them without the permission of the breeder.

The litter and their surroundings should be spotlessly clean, and the mother should also be available for you to see and to observe her temperament. Do not expect her to be in pristine condition – after rearing a litter, she will undoubtedly have lost weight and probably be in poor coat. Once the puppies have been completely weaned, usually by six weeks of age, mother will gradually regain her figure and come back into coat. Sometimes you can see the sire (father), but often a top-winning dog from another kennel has been used and may live many miles away. You can ask to see a photograph of him, or you may decide to visit a show that he is attending, where you can see him performing in the ring.

After a few minutes of initial shyness, the puppies should be outgoing and eager to play with

CHOOSING A BULLDOG

Watch the puppies
playing together to get
an idea of their
individual characters.

you – shoelaces are their first targets! They should be used to being handled and should already be socialised. If they have been reared in the house, they will be used to all the household noises, such as the washing machine, vacuum cleaner, telephone, TV etc. Look for bright, clear eyes, clean ears and tails, short nails and shining coats. They should have chunky, solid bodies – but they should not be so fat that they cannot stand and run around. Lightweight puppies with balloon-like, distended stomachs have probably not been wormed properly.

If you are not completely happy with the litter, their surroundings or the owners, do not be tempted to purchase one of the pups. Feeling sorry for them is the wrong reason to buy. It encourages bad breeders and could leave you with a sickly puppy. I have heard many horror stories from disappointed new owners who ring me for advice. When I ask if they have contacted the breeder, the answer is always the same – that the breeder does not want to know. Often, the new owners have not even seen the conditions in which the puppy had been kept before they bought

him. They probably paid the same price as they would to a reputable, experienced breeder, who is willing to give all the advice from years of experience and also after-care assistance, which is invaluable in a crisis.

You must be prepared to be vetted by the responsible breeder. The Bulldog is a very special breed. Anyone who has spent many, many hours rearing them will want to make sure that you are buying for the right reasons, have a suitable lifestyle for a puppy, and can give him a permanent home. The most important thing to me, as a breeder, is that the puppy is going to a permanent home where he will be unconditionally loved and cared for all his life. However, should your circumstances unfortunately change at any time, always contact your breeder for help with re-homing.

PICKING A PUPPY

Colour is a matter of preference. Black is very undesirable, but red, fawn, brindle and white or any combination of these are quite acceptable. Select a puppy with a smooth coat, plenty of loose skin, straight bone in the front legs, and tight feet. Look for one with a

Red and white.

White (with or without markings).

Fawn and white.

Brindle and white.

short back and a good spring of rib (often referred to as 'barrel ribs', meaning well rounded and deep from the shoulders down to its lowest part, where it joins the chest). He should have a brick-shaped head with depth of foreface; a wide jaw with a thumb-width between the canine teeth; small, thin rose-shaped ears; dark eyes, not too prominent; a large nose and open nostrils.

Avoid a gay tail (carried upright) or a Dudley (liver-coloured) nose. A male puppy should have two testicles descended into the scrotum (although they are not always evident at eight weeks of age).

Watch the puppies on the move and standing naturally, looking for a pleasing overall shape. Temperament is also important – if you have a young family, the bold, outgoing type may suit you. If you live alone, you may prefer the quieter, more reserved one. Quite often, a puppy chooses his owner by constantly going to them for attention, as if to say "please choose me". Use your instinct, with an equal balance of caution.

Most breeders, having spent hours caring for and watching their babies, will be able to assess which puppy they consider most suitable for your family needs. You must listen to all the advice and tips the breeder gives you, but the final choice is yours – you will know which one appeals to you the most. With luck, he will be your constant companion for many years, so be sure he is the one you really want.

MALE OR FEMALE?

You should have already decided on the sex you think will be most suitable for you and your family. Bitches are usually a little more affectionate, slightly smaller and less boisterous, but you do have to consider that they come into season on average every six months, which could be inconvenient. If you do not intend to breed from her, you may consider having her spayed. Males are slightly heavier and bigger-boned, with larger heads, and are very masculine. They seldom wander or become a problem if there are bitches in season in the area.

I am often asked which makes the best pet – a question I find difficult to answer. I always have a mixed kennel, and I find both sexes make loyal and trustworthy companions. Males

You may feel your needs are better met by an older dog.

are certainly more 'butch' and tend to stand out in a litter at eight weeks. The bitches should look feminine and be more reserved at that age.

AN OLDER DOG?

If you feel unable to cope with a very young puppy, you may prefer a slightly older Bulldog. Breeders often keep two puppies from one litter for show, because they feed better together, keep each other company, play and exercise together. Usually, by the time they are six to twelve months old, a decision is made about which one is the best show prospect. The other one is then available to a good pet home. At this age, he

will be lead-trained and house-trained, although you must expect a few accidents until he gets used to his new surroundings and routine. You should make sure you are given his veterinary card with the dates of his inoculations and worming.

The other alternative is a rescue Bulldog. These are dogs of various ages that have to be re-homed due to marriage break-ups, financial difficulties or even death. The dog is taken in, his requirements are assessed and he is thoroughly checked over by a veterinary surgeon. Every precaution is taken to match each unfortunate dog with a suitable owner. It is vital that this second move is a

Plastic beds are easy to clean.

permanent one, so you must be prepared for a thorough vetting. Your national Kennel Club can provide details of Bulldog rescue centres in your area.

PREPARATIONS

As with any addition to the household, there are preparations to be made. Firstly, decide where the Bulldog puppy is going to sleep and spend time while you are out. The kitchen or utility room are ideal, especially if the floors are washable – there is bound to be the occasional accident until he is fully house-trained. Start saving your old newspapers! Baby stair-gates can be very useful – you can then confine him to one room for short periods when necessary, but you will still be able to see and talk to him. You can also prepare yourself for your new arrival by purchasing the equipment he will need, puppy-proofing your property and finding a vet before you collect him.

EQUIPMENT

There are many pet superstores with a huge selection of equipment for pets.

CHOOSING A BULLDOG

BEDS AND BEDDING

Your puppy's first requirement is a warm, strong bed. When buying one, remember that Bulldog puppies grow very quickly; if you buy a bed that fits him at eight weeks of age, it will be too small in a couple of months. A larger bed with plenty of blankets is more sensible. All puppies chew, and I find the rigid plastic beds, which can be scrubbed if necessary, the most suitable. Inside, put blankets or an old sweater that you have been wearing, which seems to comfort puppies. Man-made fleece-like fabric (such as Vet-Bed) is also very popular and widely used by breeders; it washes well and is very hard-wearing. Moisture goes through the fabric and so keeps the puppy dry.

FEEDING BOWLS

The pet store will have a wide selection of food and water bowls. I find the stainless steel variety most suitable and hygienic.

COLLAR AND LEAD

You can also purchase a collar and lead, though these will not be needed for the first few weeks. Huge, wide leather or studded collars are not necessary, and they are uncomfortable for the dog. I find the woven nylon collars excellent; they have a metal buckle, with a spike that you can push through the webbing to make a perfect fit. There is a selection of woven nylon or leather leads to match these collars.

TOYS

Doggie toys and nylon bones will

Choose toys that are both safe and durable.

be useful in the early days, but make sure they are the correct ones for puppies.

CRATE

If you intend to travel frequently or to show your Bulldog, it is a good idea to get him used to a travel crate, which will make travelling much safer. The wire crates can be collapsed and folded away when not in use. Always purchase a good-quality one, as some of the cheaper types are a false economy. The size I use for an adult is approximately 31 ins (79 cms) long, 21 ins (53 cms) wide and 24 ins (61 cms) high. If

An indoor crate can also be used in the car.

you start him young and use the crate for short periods, your Bulldog pup will soon get used to being shut in. You will find that once he is accustomed to his little house, he will be happy to sleep there for short periods, but never keep him shut in for too long.

OUTSIDE KENNELS

You may want the option of being able to keep your Bulldog in an outside kennel occasionally – especially if you intend to have more than one dog.

I prefer wooden kennels, as they always seem warmer than brick or concrete. If they are lined with hardboard, it helps to eliminate the cold, and the smooth interior discourages chewing. Some dogs are determined to find something to chew, usually their doorway. If this happens, put a metal strip around the opening. My kennels are located in a position where I can see them from my kitchen window. They must be rain-proofed, and must have access to shade in the summer. The kennel should open into a covered concrete or gravel run, measuring approximately twelve feet by six feet (four metres by two metres), so the dogs can go in and out at will.

If you decide you want him to

Make sure your garden is puppy-proofed – Bulldog puppies are great explorers.

spend time in a kennel, get him used to it in the warm weather, so that, by the time winter comes, he will have gradually become accustomed to a drop in temperature. As I said earlier, a Bulldog is placid and quiet – he is unlikely to bark constantly and annoy your neighbours.

PUPPY-PROOFING

Check that your garden is properly fenced. Although adult Bulldogs seldom wander, a young puppy is inquisitive and may decide to explore. It is surprising what small gaps puppies can squeeze through. Inspect your gates – some have a gap underneath big enough for a puppy to crawl through. Wrought-iron gates can be a hazard. It is a good idea to put fine-mesh wire on the bottom section, which stops feet getting caught in the

curly patterns. I also have a warning sign on my gate saying 'Dogs running free'. These signs are on sale at pet stores and at dog shows. Not only are they a safeguard for visitors, but they also warn off intruders, especially if they include a picture of a Bulldog showing his teeth!

Swimming pools should be out of bounds for your puppy, as there have been rare instances of Bulldogs drowning.

FINDING A VET

If you have never had a pet before and have no knowledge of the vets in your area, do a little research in advance. Ask established breeders or friends with pets for recommendations, and, if possible, try to find a vet who has knowledge of, and experience with, Bulldogs.

4 *Puppy Care*

Before you collect your puppy, make a list of all the questions you wish to ask, because, when you see him, you will probably be very excited and forget everything you intended to discuss with the breeder. If you have a written list, you can check any queries you may have. A dedicated breeder will want to give you all the help and advice he can.

COLLECTING YOUR PUPPY

If possible, collect the puppy in the morning, and he will then have the rest of the day to settle into his new surroundings before bedtime.

Take an old towel and some kitchen roll in case your puppy is travel-sick – he may never have been in a car before. It is a good idea to take a friend with you so that they can drive. The puppy can then sit on your lap, where he can be reassured. I never feed puppies before they leave for a new home, as this helps to avoid car-sickness, and it is a good idea for him to arrive at his new home feeling hungry. He will settle happily when he sees his food!

Your breeder should provide a diet sheet, and I always prepare a couple of meals of their usual food for my puppies' new owners to take home with them. Make sure you stick to the same diet for the first few days; puppies easily get upset tummies if their diet is changed suddenly. If you eventually wish to alter the diet, do it very gradually, by adding a little of the new food to each meal and increasing the amount over four to five days until the changeover is complete.

I always give a few written instructions on puppy rearing, together with worming and vaccination details. You should also receive his pedigree and registration documents. The

The great day arrives when you take your puppy home.

puppy may come insured for the first six weeks. I would always advise you to continue the policy, or to obtain a quote from another company. It can be money well spent.

Ask to be shown the correct way to lift your puppy. Bulldogs are heavy and awkward to pick up because they wriggle so much, so you must have a secure hold. I approach from the side, put one arm under the chin and the other arm under the tummy, and scoop up. Never allow young children to try to pick him up – serious

damage can occur from wrong handling.

SETTLING IN

When you arrive home, give your puppy time to get accustomed to his new surroundings. It is not a good idea to have family, friends and neighbours around too early – the puppy needs time to adjust and to explore the house and garden. Introduce him to any other animals in the family carefully, so no one feels left out. If you have young children, make sure they do not pick him up or

Give your puppy a chance to explore his new surroundings.

tire him out. Young puppies need lots of rest, and your children must learn to respect this. *Never* leave young children unattended with a puppy – accidents can happen, and prevention is the best remedy.

SLEEPING

I cannot stress enough how important it is to allow your Bulldog plenty of sleep as a young puppy. You should have already decided where he is going to sleep – maybe in the kitchen or the utility room, but somewhere draught-free and warm. He will miss his littermates and will probably cry for a couple of nights. You may have to get up to reassure him, but do not fall into the trap of taking him to your bedroom; it

is a habit you will find difficult to break.

There are many ideas for helping your Bulldog puppy to settle on his first few nights: a blanket from his breeder, which smells of his littermates; an old sweater you have been wearing; a stone hot-water-bottle; a ticking clock; music playing – any of these things may help, but it may be a case of 'grin and bear it'. Be patient with him; it is a big change in his life and routine, and he will feel insecure at first. However, you will find that Bulldogs have a very placid and adaptable nature, and they soon settle into their new homes. Given affection and a regular routine, your puppy will soon become one of the family and fit in with your lifestyle.

FEEDING

Weather permitting, feed your puppy outside, as all puppies relieve themselves straight after a meal. Bulldogs can be very messy eaters – they tend to put their entire face into the bowl and spread their food everywhere. By getting your Bulldog into the habit of feeding outside, you will save yourself a great deal of cleaning up.

At eight weeks of age, your puppy will be having five meals a day. A typical diet would probably be:

7 am
Eggs (two, scrambled or hard-boiled) or plain breakfast cereal with milk. Never give cow's milk. I use diluted evaporated milk (three parts milk to one part water) or a formulation especially for puppies, obtained from your vet.

11 am
About 4 oz raw minced (chopped) beef with 2 oz fine puppy mixer.

3 pm
As above. Occasionally, replace with 4 oz cooked chicken or fish and a little grated cheese.

7 pm
Cereal, rice pudding, scrambled eggs, or any variety of dried food suitable for puppies. Follow the directions on the pack, which tell you how much to feed according to the weight of your puppy.

10.30pm
Meat and biscuit (as at 11am).

Add bone-meal or vitamins once a day.

It is important to keep the feeding times regular. Never miss a meal and then give double the next time – you will be asking for a tummy upset. It soon becomes obvious that your puppy prefers the meat meals to the milky ones.

Too much milk can cause loose motions – if this happens, cut out milk completely. By the time your puppy is ten weeks old, reduce the number of meals to four per day. At 16 weeks, he should be on three meals per day, and at six

Bulldogs are rarely fussy about their food.

months, two meals. Increase the amount of good-quality food as required.

Bulldogs are greedy puppies, and it is rare to have a poor eater, but their appetites vary, so it is always difficult to say exactly how large a meal to feed. As a rough guide, at six months, he will probably eat about 1 lb of meat per day, plus almost half the quantity of mixer biscuit. Chopped raw carrot or cabbage can also be added occasionally. If a dog has cleared his dish quickly and is looking for more, I give a little extra at the next meal. If he is leaving food, you are giving too much. Never leave food down; give him ample time to eat what he wants, pick the remainder up and make him wait for his next meal.

Between the age of 12 and 18 months, I find that Bulldogs are happy with one meal a day, which I always feed in the evening. Some people prefer to feed two smaller meals – one in the morning and one at night – but, as your Bulldog grows, you will discover what suits him best. Do not forget to have a clean bowl of water available at all times, and this should be refreshed twice a day.

TYPES OF FOOD
The type of food you use is a personal choice, but good food (and plenty of it) is essential for a strong, healthy Bulldog. There is an old saying that 80 per cent of your Champion goes in his mouth. My puppies are reared on best minced (chopped) beef with biscuit, fish, eggs and evaporated milk. The adults have tripe and

mixer biscuit. Although dogs love it, you may find the raw green tripe smelly and unpleasant to handle, especially in the summer. Pet stores and supermarkets sell a huge variety of canned dog food, which, served with biscuit mixer, is perfectly adequate for your Bulldog.

Many people prefer to use an all-in-one dried food, and there is a wide variety to choose from at all pet stores. If you use dried food, read the instructions carefully and follow the guidelines regarding the amounts required for your size of dog. However, remember that these are only average suggestions; each dog is individual and, like people, requires a slightly different amount to maintain condition. These foods normally contain all the necessary vitamins, so do not feed extra, but always remember that plenty of fresh water must be available at all times.

FEEDING TIPS

Never feed your Bulldog tidbits from your table. There is nothing worse than a dribbling puppy worrying you throughout your meal. If you do not ever start it, he will never expect it.

Never feed chicken bones or any small bones that may splinter. Only feed pork occasionally.

A lean dog is a healthy dog – make sure you keep your Bulldog at the correct weight.

Never feed chocolate. Theobromine is contained in cocoa, and its derivatives can be fatal to animals. It was originally believed that it had to be consumed in large quantities for it to kill, but recent evidence suggests that 1 oz of dark chocolate can have disastrous results.

Remember – a male adult Bulldog should weigh 55 lbs, and a female 50 lbs. Do not allow yours to become overweight. You are not being kind to your pets if they are unable to exercise freely.

HOUSE-TRAINING

Put newspaper down at night because your puppy will probably not be clean all night, for the first few weeks at least. I start with the newspaper near his bed and over the course of a few days gradually move it nearer to the door. This helps him to recognise where he is expected to go, and, if the door is open during the day, he will soon learn to go outside.

Always put your puppy outside as soon as he wakes in the morning, and then regularly thoughout the day – at least every two hours. Praise him when he is clean. The more time you spend with him, the quicker you will have him house-trained. If you watch your puppy, you will soon recognise the signs that he wants to go – nose down, going round in circles, looking for the 'right' spot. Quickly put him outside, and, when he has been to the toilet, tell him what a good boy he is and allow him back into the

If you take your puppy out regularly, accidents should be kept to a minimum

Bulldogs are not Greyhounds – but they do enjoy their exercise.

house. With time and patience, your puppy will soon get the message and will let you know when he wants to go out.

EXERCISE

Do not over-exercise your puppy. I do not start road-walking my puppies until they reach about five months of age. Start with short distances and build up to a distance that suits him. It is a myth that Bulldogs do not need exercising. All dogs need exercise and, provided you build up the distance gradually, most Bulldogs are capable of two miles a day – some, even more. However, remember he is a Bulldog, and he will never run like a Greyhound or retrieve like a gundog. It is most important that you do not take your Bulldog out walking in the heat of the day. In the summer, walk him early in the morning and late in the evening, but never straight after he has eaten.

HEALTH CHECK

It is advisable to give the puppy a couple of days to settle into his new surroundings and then take him to your vet for a thorough examination and health check. If there are any problems, contact the breeder immediately. All dedicated breeders are concerned about their babies – they have spent a tremendous amount of time rearing them. I am sure that, like me, your breeder will greatly appreciate a quick telephone call with news that the puppy has settled into his new home and is loved by all the family.

VACCINATION

Veterinary opinion seems to differ regarding the best time to inoculate against killer diseases such as parvovirus, distemper, canine hepatitis and leptospirosis. Take the advice of your own vet. Remember that you must not allow your puppy in parks, on the street or to meet any strange dogs until his course of injections is complete and your vet has given the all-clear. However, he can play in your garden or with your pets, provided they have been inoculated.

WORMING

All puppies and adult dogs should be wormed regularly. Your puppy should already have been wormed and you should have been given the dates. Make sure you ask your vet for further worming advice. It is a very simple process, consisting of either a crushed tablet in his food or a spoonful of liquid, with the dosage depending on the weight of the puppy. All instructions come with the preparation.

GROOMING

Bulldogs are extremely easy to maintain, but start as you mean to go on and get him used to being groomed regularly. Make it an enjoyable event, with a little reward, such as a piece of cheese, when the routine has been completed. As a puppy, he can stand on a table on a mat – the small sample carpet squares are ideal; they give the puppy grip and make him feel secure. Brush him with a bristle brush or a rubber pad to remove dead hair, and check his skin for any blemish or soreness. You can bath him occasionally if you really feel the need, but I find that regular brushing keeps the coat clean and gives it a lovely shiny gloss. Bathing too often removes the natural oils, which help to repel the dirt.

Pay particular attention to the nose roll (also known as 'nose rope'), facial creases and tail. Some dogs have a rather heavy nose rope, and this can become infected if it is not kept clean. It is especially important in hot weather, when the creases can become moist and sore if not attended to. I find baby wet-wipes very useful for cleaning the creases, eyes and face, and if there is any soreness, petroleum jelly is a good remedy. The nose can sometimes become crusty, and petroleum jelly or coconut oil rubbed in every few days will cure this.

Ears are seldom a problem with

PUPPY CARE AND GROOMING

Accustom your puppy to being groomed from an early age.

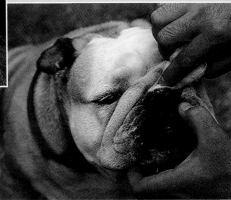

The nose roll must be kept clean.

Ears may need cleaning, but make sure you do not probe too deeply.

Regular tooth-brushing will ensure that tartar does not accumulate on the teeth.

Bulldogs, because the rose ear allows air to circulate. If they do appear dirty, clean with cotton wool (cotton), but never poke deep into the ear.

Some dogs have a tight or screw tail, and this must be kept clean and treated with medicated powder to avoid infection.

NAIL CARE

You will probably have to trim your puppy's nails, but as soon as you start to road-walk him, you will find that his nails will wear down on the hard surface. However, you must occasionally check his dewclaws, which are fifth toes, in the thumb position,

slightly higher than the other four toes on his front paws. Because they do not touch the ground as the dog walks, they are never worn down, so they must be trimmed to avoid them growing back into the flesh.

You must take care not to cut your Bulldog's nails too short and to avoid the quick, as this will bleed and be painful for him. If he has white nails, it is easy to see the pink section that you must avoid, but if his nails are black, it is more difficult. In these cases, just nip off the tip and do it regularly.

Once again, start as you mean to go on. If you get him used to

Guillotine-type nail clippers can be used to keep your Bulldog's nails in trim.

Dogs need routine – and the Bulldog is no exception.

clippers at an early age, you will not have a problem in later life.

ROUTINE

The most important thing for any dog is to have a routine. He will soon learn and accept your way of life, as long as it is consistent. Most problems arise when dogs do not know from one day to the next when or where they are going to sleep, be fed and walked, played with, etc.

Do not fall into the trap of thinking that you cannot go out because of the puppy. If he has been exercised, fed and played with, then it is perfectly acceptable to leave him in his bed while you do your own thing.

5 *Training*

As I have said before, Bulldogs are known for being stubborn and obstinate – they are not dogs who jump to attention each time you call. They appear to consider your request carefully before deciding if they want to obey. So, it is vital that you start as you mean to go on, and teach him your house rules from day one. If you want an easy-to-train, obedient dog, then the Bulldog is not for you. However, it is this side of the dog's nature that appeals to many owners. The placid, laid-back temperament with that sour expression that seems to say "I will come when I am ready" fascinates lovers of the breed. If you are prepared to be patient and persistent, you will have the most loyal companion, who will always want to be by your side.

It is important to start training your puppy early. Give him a week to settle in to his new home and routine, then start with short lessons throughout the day. Make it a fun time, enjoyable for both you and your puppy. He will learn and obey much more quickly if he is happy and can sense that you are pleased with him. Try to finish each session with success, and praise him generously. Keep all the command words simple – "Come", "Sit", "Down", "No" – using your tone of voice for emphasis.

Your Bulldog must learn who is boss. Never allow him to dominate you or any member of the family – he has to fit in with your routine. A puppy training class is always worth attending to help socialise your Bulldog with other dogs and to master basic obedience.

COMING WHEN CALLED
Firstly, your Bulldog must be trained to come when called. A small reward, such as a piece of cheese, with generous praise and

TRAINING

Your Bulldog must learn his place, and live in harmony with all members of the family.

Make yourself sound exciting so that your dog wants to come to you.

patting, will encourage him. Never shout or smack him. If you feel he is becoming bored with the lesson, stop, and resume later on.

Allow him off the lead in your garden for some free exercise. You will probably find that, when you call him, he will wander off in the opposite direction. Never run after him – he will think it is a fun game and will have you chasing him around to see who tires first! It is better to crouch at his level and to call him by name, and if that does not work, casually walk away from him towards the house. It will not take long for him to realise that he is being left behind, and he will soon be by your side. Once again, fuss and praise

him – if you chastise him, he may be afraid to return to you next time.

SIT

Teaching your Bulldog to sit is easier. Say the word "Sit" and, at the same time, press on his rear until he obliges. After a few attempts, you should have success. However, if you intend to show your dog, never teach him to sit until he is fully show-trained. A show dog must be taught to stand in a show stance and is never required to sit in the ring.

LEAVE

"Leave" is an important command to teach a Bulldog. As soon as you have him, practise taking toys, bones or chews from his mouth, saying the word "Leave". After a few seconds, make a big fuss of him, telling him how clever he is, and then give them back to him. This is an essential lesson for your Bulldog to learn, especially if you have young children, who may suddenly decide to grab his toys. Should there be any adverse reaction from him, immediately rebuke him with a stern voice.

Your puppy must learn to give up his toy when you ask him to "Leave".

DOWN

It is most important to train your Bulldog not to jump up. When he is a puppy, it may seem like fun, but as he gets older and heavier, it is unacceptable. A dog of 50-60 lbs will easily knock over a child or an elderly person. From the first day, you may have to reprimand him. "No" or "Down" is usually sufficient – it is the tone of voice that is important. A short sharp "Down" in a deep voice will soon be understood. Then praise him in a softer tone, with a pat on his head to tell him he is a good boy.

If your Bulldog attempts to jump on to your furniture, immediately say "Down" and point to the floor or to his bed. He will soon learn your hand signals, so, when you point to his bed, he will know his place.

NO MEANS NO

The 'No' command is self-explanatory. Your tone of voice is very important. Here, as with all your training, you must be consistent. It is no good punishing your Bulldog one day, and allowing him to get away with the same thing the following day. Most badly-behaved dogs are the product of bad owners, so make sure yours is well trained and popular with your friends and neighbours.

MOUTHING AND CHEWING

Do not allow your puppy to bite or nibble your hands or feet. The Bulldog's teeth are like needles, and, apart from the damage they can do, it will be very painful. A tap on the nose and "No!" is all that is required.

Do not give him an old slipper or shoe to play with and chew; he will not understand the difference between a discarded shoe and your latest new pair! There are numerous toys manufactured for pets, which are safe for your puppy to play with, but make sure that they are too big for him to swallow, and, if he does start to chew them up, take them away. Large marrowbones are useful when he is teething and to keep him amused. I always feed them raw, but watch that they do not splinter, because that can be dangerous. As soon as they start looking ragged, take them away.

Practise taking bones or toys away from your puppy. Talk to him and stroke him, then ask him to release the object, saying "Leave" or "Thank you". He should willingly let go; you can

then praise him, and, after a few minutes, give the object back to him.

In the interests of hygiene, you should also stop your Bulldog from licking people's faces.

LEAD-TRAINING

Lead-training can be frustrating, because of the Bulldog's stubbornness. When they are two to three months old, I put a small, soft collar on my Bulldogs for a short period each day. This helps your puppy to get used to the feeling of something around his neck, and, when you attach a lead a few weeks later, it is not quite such a shock. Do not make it too tight – it should be just tight enough to stop it from slipping over his head. The puppy grows at a tremendous rate at this early age, and you will find you can adjust the fit for several weeks.

Start walking your Bulldog around the garden. He will probably refuse to move at first, but a little coaxing and tempting with a tidbit will help. Never try to pull or drag him along, as this will only make him more determined to dig his heels in! If you have an older dog or a child, you will find he will be more likely to walk at their side.

With gentle encouragement, lead-training should pose few problems.

Later, when he has been trained to walk reliably on a collar and lead, you may prefer to use a slip lead. I find these perfectly adequate, because properly trained Bulldogs seldom pull – they are happy to amble beside you. If you prefer a leather collar and lead, a one-inch to one-and-a-half-inch width is the most suitable. Although I have seen Bulldogs wearing harnesses, I have never found one necessary.

VENTURING OUT

As soon as your puppy is happy walking around the garden on a lead, you can venture a little further afield. The first time you go near traffic, he may be nervous. Stand on the pavement for a few minutes; talk to him and stroke him, reassuring him as cars pass by. Gradually, he will gain confidence and ignore the noisy traffic. Persevere, as a well-trained dog will be a credit to you.

Do not forget to fit an identification disc. A small tag on his collar with your surname and telephone number is all that is required. Alternatively, you may

Ring training classes are available if you plan to show your Bulldog.

consider having him microchipped or tattooed. Your vet will advise you on these options.

When out walking, always remember to take a couple of plastic bags in your pocket. You are responsible for cleaning up after your dog. You clean up at home and you must do the same wherever you are, in the interest of hygiene and in consideration for the general public.

It is a good idea to get your puppy used to travelling in the car as early as possible. Start with regular short journeys, and you will find he enjoys the outing.

TRAINING CLASSES

It is a good idea to take your Bulldog to training classes. These are for general behaviour, such as walking to heel, Sit and Stay commands, and, of course, for socialising. Make it a pleasurable outing for you and your Bulldog, as he will learn much quicker if he is enjoying himself. Remember – unruly dogs are not popular and can be a nuisance to your friends and neighbours.

AGILITY

Some Bulldogs take part in Agility, which consists of a series of obstacles, such as jumps, tunnels and weaving poles. It is not something I have had experience in, but I have friends who have had great fun and limited success.

A Bulldog is never going to excel in such an event. Because of his weight and build, he does not have the ability to run and turn as fast as most of his opponents. If you are interested in this type of hobby, start your puppy early, do not allow him to become overweight and keep him fit and well exercised. Never expect him to perform in hot weather, and, if he appears to be struggling at any time, allow him to retire.

Build up your training programme gradually, and your fellow competitors may be pleasantly surprised how well your dog can perform. Do keep some perspective, however – you can never compare a Bulldog's performance with a working dog's. The purpose of attending these occasions should be for you and your Bulldog to have a fun day out.

6

The Show Bulldog

All pedigree breeds have what is called a Breed Standard, which describes all the points of the perfect dog. We all know that the 'perfect' dog does not exist, but dedicated breeders strive to achieve a specimen as close to the ideal as possible. Judges examine each exhibit and assess its various qualities, before placing them in order of merit, as they see them on the day. No two judges interpret the Standard in the same way, so results can vary on different days with different judges.

THE BULLDOG STANDARD

Compared to most breeds, the Bulldog Standard is quite complex, and has changed very little since 1865. The basic requirements then were for a courageous dog that crouched low to the ground, and had strong shoulders and body to enable him to pin the bull, and lighter hindquarters for agility. He would have a strong jaw to grip and hold, and would convey an impression of determination and strength similar to that of a thickset Ayrshire Bull.

The Bulldog's general appearance should be of a smooth-coated, thickset dog, rather low in stature. He should have heavy bone, a broad front, with hindquarters high and strong, but lighter than his foreparts. His body should be short and his limbs should be stout and muscular. The following is a simplified version of the UK Standard.

CHARACTERISTICS
The Bulldog should convey an impression of determination, strength and activity.

TEMPERAMENT
He should be alert, bold, loyal, dependable, courageous and fierce

The distinctive Bulldog head is broad and wrinkled.

in appearance, but he should possess an affectionate nature.

HEAD

The Bulldog is termed a 'head' breed – the head being of utmost importance. It should be large, very broad and square, and wrinkled. The muzzle is short, wide and turned upwards (termed 'upsweep'), and very deep from the corner of the eye to the corner of the mouth. The nose should be large, broad and black – never liver-coloured, red or brown. The nostrils are large and wide, with a well-defined vertical line between. The jaws should be broad, massive and square, with the lower jaw projecting considerably in front of the upper jaw – termed 'undershot'. Another characteristic is the Bulldog's 'chops' or 'flews' – his low-hanging cheeks. These are thick, very broad, and overhang the lower jaw on either side.

EYES

The eyes should be very dark and show no white when looking forward. They should be round and of moderate size, set well apart.

EARS

The shape of the ear is termed 'rose ear'. It should be small and thin, folding inwards at the back, with the upper or front edge curving outwards and backwards, showing part of the inside ear.

MOUTH

The jaws must be broad and square, with six small front teeth between the canines. The canines must be wide apart. It is important that the lower jaw is parallel with the upper jaw, and that the teeth cannot be seen when the mouth is closed.

NECK

Moderate in length, very thick and strong, well arched at the back, with loose, thick and wrinkled skin at the throat.

FOREQUARTERS

The shoulders should be broad, muscular and very powerful; they should give the appearance of being 'tacked on' to the body. The brisket (chest) must be deep to allow room for lung development. The front legs should be very stout and strong, set wide apart.

The forequarters are muscular and very powerful.

The body is short and strong, and is described as pear-shaped.

BODY

The back should be short and strong, broad at the shoulder and comparatively narrow at the loins (termed 'pear-shaped'). The chest is wide and deep, and the ribs well rounded. There should be a slight fall to the back, close behind the shoulders, and the spine should then rise to the loins, the top of which should be higher than the shoulders, then curve to the tail, forming an arch. This is termed 'roach back' – an important feature of the Bulldog.

HINDQUARTERS

The hind legs should be large and muscular, and longer in proportion than the front legs, so as to elevate the loins. The lower part of the leg should be short, straight and strong, with stifles turning slightly outwards, away from the body. The hocks, therefore, approach each other, and the hind feet turn outwards.

The 'Bulldog roll' is a characteristic of the breed.

FEET

The front feet should be medium-sized and round, and should turn very slightly outwards. The back feet should be round and compact, with toes split up and knuckles prominent.

TAIL

The tail should be low-set and straight. It should be thick at the root, tapering quickly to a fine point, but never carried above the back. Many dogs now have screw tails, and these are accepted in the show ring.

MOVEMENT

The Bulldog has an unusual movement, often called 'the Bulldog roll'. It is particularly heavy and constrained. He takes short, quick steps on the tips of his toes with his hind feet skimming the ground.

COAT

Fine-textured, short, close and smooth; never wiry.

COLOUR

Whole or smut (whole colour with black mask or muzzle). Brindle, red, fawn, fallow, white or white with any combination of these colours. Dudley, black, and black and tan are highly undesirable.

SIZE

Dogs 25 kgs (55 lbs). Bitches 22.7 kgs (50 lbs).
All males should have two testicles fully descended into the scrotum.

THE AKC STANDARD

The AKC (American Kennel Club) Standard is based on the UK Standard. The most obvious difference is in the size. The AKC states: 'The size for mature dogs is about 50lbs; for mature bitches about 40lbs'. The AKC also gives preference to colour in the following order: 1.) red brindle, 2.) all other brindles, 3.) solid white, 4.) solid red, fawn, and fallow, 5.) piebald, 6.) inferior qualities of all the foregoing. Movement is described differently in the AKC, too. The action must be 'unrestrained, free and vigorous'.

GETTING STARTED

If you are interested in showing your Bulldog, non-Championship local shows are a good place to start with your puppy. These can be charity events, often held in conjunction with a local fete or carnival. It will be a very informal atmosphere, and very much a fun day. These events can usually be entered on the day. Before you start, you will need to train your Bulldog to prepare him for the ring.

Dog showing can become a very compulsive hobby.

Dog showing can be a pleasurable hobby, as long as it is kept in perspective. Remember, you always take the best dog home!

PREPARATION

Bulldogs are relatively easy to show because they require very little preparation. They may need the occasional bath, particularly if they are predominantly white, but certainly not the hours spent on long-coated or trimmed breeds. If you regularly brush your Bulldog, he will have a clean, shiny coat, which you can enhance by rubbing it with chamois leather or a velvet pad. Check all the wrinkles are clean and dry, and try to avoid any eye staining by wiping the eyes daily. Make sure that his ears are clean and that his nails are short.

TRAINING FOR THE SHOW RING

Training must start from an early age. I stand my puppies on a table (as I described for grooming) every day from the age of six weeks. Just a few minutes are all that is necessary to begin with.

At first, it is not important how the legs and feet are placed; just concentrate on getting him to stand still, while you continuously stroke and fuss him. Talk to him all the time and tell him to stand. Gradually, as he relaxes, you will be able to move his legs into the correct position. Put your hand under his chin and place his front legs, but do not stand them too wide – you are aiming for a square shape, when viewed from the front. The back legs should be slightly closer together, so that, when viewed from the front, the back legs can be seen between the front legs. It is a good idea to place your Bulldog in front of a mirror – you can then see a complete picture, as a judge would see him. You must have endless patience and make it a happy time for him with a reward at the end of each session.

After all your puppy's vaccinations are completed, you can join your local ring training classes. The secretary of your nearest dog club will be able to tell you when and where they are held, or there may be details in your veterinary surgery. Some clubs prefer puppies to be over a certain age before they start training.

The first time you attend, it is a good idea to just sit and watch. You can learn a great deal from the experienced handlers, and your

THE SHOW BULLDOG

Place the outer front leg.

Place the inner front leg.

Position the hind legs.

The final result: a perfect stand.

puppy can become accustomed to the other dogs and new surroundings before making his debut. You will learn how to present your puppy in the show ring, how to stand and how to walk him correctly. Bulldogs are always exhibited front-on, facing the judge; most other breeds stand sideways. If there are no other Bulldogs at your ring training class, make sure the instructor knows the correct stance for your breed.

Before entering any shows, your Bulldog must be well socialised with other dogs and used to being handled by strangers. Practise at home – ask your friends to go over him, look in his mouth, etc. When he is six months old, you can enter him in a show. The dog papers advertise all forthcoming shows, and your ring training classes may also have schedules of local shows. However, it is pointless going into the show ring if your Bulldog will not behave correctly. You may have the best dog in the class, but if he does not allow the judge to handle him, or if he refuses to walk, his chances of being placed are slim. Do not rush to get him into the big show ring. Be patient and refrain from entering any breed shows until you are confident that you are both ready.

Prepare your Bulldog for the show ring by practising his show stance, and getting him used to being inspected thoroughly.

GLOSSARY OF TERMS

The following is a list of terms you may encounter when discussing the Bulldog.

APPLE HEAD: Rounded or domed skull.

BARREL RIBS: Rounded, almost circular in contour.

BRISKET: The anterior part of the ribcage between the front legs.

BUTTON EARS: Semi-erect ears with the tip dropping forward.

CHOPS: Pendulous lips.

CRYPTORCHID: A male without testicles.

FLEWS: Pendulous lips and cheeks.

FURROW: The line running up the centre of the dog's forehead.

GAY TAIL: A tail carried too high over the back.

LEVEL BITE: When the teeth meet edge to edge.

MASK: Dark shading on the foreface.

MONORCHID: A male with only one testicle.

MUZZLE: The foreface and facial assembly, including the mouth.

OUT AT ELBOW: When the elbows protrude, standing or moving.

PADDLING: Moving wide in the front with the feet turned out.

SCREW TAIL: A distorted or twisted tail.

SHORT COUPLED: Short and strong in the loins.

SLAB SIDED: Flat in the ribs.

SNIPEY: Narrow and shallow in the muzzle.

SWAY BACK: A dipping back line.

TOP LINE: The profile of the dog's upper outline from the back of the head to the tail.

TUCK UP: The upward curve under the dog's belly.

TURN UP: When the underjaw is turned up.

WRY JAW: When the upper and lower jaws fail to meet in parallel alignment.

7 *Breeding*

Think carefully before deciding to mate your bitch. Bulldogs are not easy when it comes to breeding. You should talk to some experienced breeders and ask for their opinions and guidance. Do not believe the old saying that it will do your bitch good to have a litter. I know plenty of Bulldogs that have lived long, healthy, happy lives without producing puppies. However, if you still feel it is what you want for your bitch, ask yourself the following questions:

1 Are you prepared to give her 24-hour attention for the first two to three weeks after the birth, and do you have a supportive and understanding family? Bulldogs are clumsy – they can easily sit or lie on their newborn babies and suffocate them. It is vital that they are never left unattended.

2 Have you the facilities in your home to cope with a litter of growing puppies until you can find the right homes for them? Are you prepared to take back any puppies that you sell, any time they need re-homing?

3 Do you have an understanding vet who is sympathetic to Bulldogs, and are you prepared to risk your bitch if she requires a Caesarean?

Next, you must consider the expense: the stud fee, plus travelling costs to visit the dog; the possibility of a large vet bill; food costs – both mother and babies will require plenty of the best-quality food; heating bills – warmth is of the utmost importance, and the puppies will need to be kept at a constant temperature of approximately 75 to 80 degrees F for the first few

*Think very carefully before taking on the challenge of breeding Bulldogs.
Photo: Sally Anne Thompson.*

weeks. You will also need a reliable washing machine – you will find that it is in constant use until the puppies are ready to leave home.

Your bitch should be in good health, have no hereditary problems, be fit and active and not overweight. Never mate her on her first season. By her second season, she should be well over a year old and mature enough to cope with a litter. If possible, consult the person who bred her, or an experienced judge of the breed, to confirm that she is suitable for reproduction.

FINDING A STUD DOG

Ask your bitch's breeder for advice about stud dogs with a pedigree compatible with hers. Go to a few shows, look at the dogs recommended and make your choice. All this must, of course, take place before she comes into season.

Approach the stud dog owner to enquire about the stud fee, and to see if he is willing to let you use his dog. The fee must be paid when the mating is completed. The stud dog requires experienced handling, so do not be tempted to use the dog down the road, if he or his owners have no experience. If you have a novice handler with an unproved dog, it is unlikely that a satisfactory mating will be

If you have dogs and bitches in the house, they will have to be separated when the bitch comes into season.

achieved with your maiden bitch. There is a definite art in handling a stud dog – the experienced will make it look simple and will cause no stress to your bitch.

THE SEASON

Bulldog bitches can come into season any time after they reach six months of age, but usually not until they are eight or nine months old. The vulva will swell up, and she will discharge red blood for approximately ten days. The colour will gradually lighten to pale pink, followed by a straw tinge – when, for the next four to eight days, she will be ready for mating. The vulva will gradually shrink back to normal size, and, by day 21, her season will be over. However, all bitches are different, and Bulldogs are renowned for

having strange seasons and for being difficult to get into whelp.

If you do not want to breed from your Bulldog, it is important that you keep her away from all males during her season. This is particularly important from the ninth to the 18th day, when she is normally ready for mating and would probably accept any dog! The Bulldog is not a breed to stray or wander off, but if she has been exercised locally, you may have the neighbourhood males, who have picked up her scent, sitting on your doorstep.

If you do want to breed from your bitch, contact the stud dog owner on the first day that your bitch shows colour (day one of her season). This will enable him to make sure that his dog is available when you require him.

If you wait until the day you think she is ready, you may find that the breeder has accepted another booking.

It is important that you take your bitch to the dog on the correct day of the cycle – usually around days 10 to 14. This is only a guide, as all bitches are different, and Bulldogs can be very difficult to get into whelp. If you are unsure whether she is willing to stand (i.e. ready to accept the dog), it may be worthwhile going to your vet for a cytology test. This will confirm whether the time is right for her to be mated.

CARE OF THE BITCH IN WHELP

Just because your bitch has been mated and you have paid a fee, there is no guarantee that she will produce puppies. However, most stud dog owners allow you a free service next season if she misses. You should receive a stud form, signed by the stud dog owner, which will enable you to register the puppies with your national Kennel Club when they are born.

After mating, treat your bitch as normal, do not feed her any extra and continue her exercise. Between six and seven weeks later, it should

Bulldogs are not easy whelpers, and it takes experience to know if the bitch is going to need assistance.

become obvious if she is in whelp, and you can then start feeding a little extra. Give her two meals a day of good-quality meat and biscuit. At eight weeks, she will probably prefer three small meals a day, and her exercise will be a slow amble around the garden.

The normal gestation period is 63 days, but this is only a guide, and Bulldogs often produce early. I always like to inform my vet if I have a bitch in whelp at least a week before the puppies are due, just in case there is a problem. It is preferable that your bitch and her puppies are kept in a room where there are no other pets or children to interfere – she will need to be kept very quiet, and to feel secure. You will need to position a large whelping box in her quarters at least a week before the puppies are due, so she is completely settled and contented before she gives birth.

Always allow your bitch a chance to self-whelp. Far too many Caesareans occur because owners panic and do not give the bitch enough time.

FURTHER STUDY

As I have said, the Bulldog is a very complicated breed, unless you have had some experience with them. I do not feel they are suitable for the novice breeder.

There are many books you can study to give you a wider insight into breeding dogs. Booklets are also available via any of the Bulldog breed clubs – contact your national Kennel Club for

The whelping box must be large, with 'pig rails' to ensure the bitch does not squash her fragile puppies.

The rewards of rearing a litter are great – but it should not be undertaken by a novice owner.

details. I do stress that this absorbing, pleasurable hobby can be an expensive, heartbreaking experience. Anyone who has bred Bulldogs for many years has had their ups and downs – it is only the strong-willed that persevere for perfection.

SPAYING

If you do not plan to breed from your bitch, you may decide to have her spayed. This should not be carried out until she has had at least one season, and then most vets recommend that the operation is performed mid-cycle before her next season. I have never come across any adverse effect, and it certainly does not alter her temperament.

CASTRATION

There are various reasons for considering having your male dog castrated. These include: to render him sterile when he is never going to be used as a stud dog; or to help to overcome hypersexual behaviour, reducing the tendency to roam and seek out bitches in season. I have never found Bulldogs a problem when my bitches are on heat – they certainly never roam or continuously bark. The only reason I feel it necessary to castrate is if your dog has only one testicle descended. The retained testicle can become cancerous in later life, and most vets recommend removal.

8 Health Care

We are told that Bulldogs cannot breathe, walk or breed naturally, but I feel that some of the blame for this reputation should be attributed to ignorant or lazy owners. I maintain that a well-bred Bulldog, correctly fed and exercised, has no more health problems that any other dog. In fact, I would go as far as to say that he has considerably fewer than some. Over the years, my family has owned and bred many Bulldogs who have lived well into double figures and have seldom visited our vet.

Dogs rarely cry or make a fuss when they feel ill. The most obvious signs are refusing food and not wanting to come out of bed. It is often difficult to know how much your Bulldog is suffering, because they display so much courage. If you are concerned, always ask for advice from your vet. The breeder is also worth consulting, as they usually have years of experience.

All the vets I have spoken to agree that Bulldogs are the bravest animals they have treated. I have never experienced a problem with injections, operations or any other treatments – they do not even wince!

ANAL GLANDS
A common reason for problems around the tail area is blocked anal glands. The dog will scoot around on his bottom and will be generally uncomfortable. These glands are positioned on either side of the anus and may require emptying. This is not an easy job for the novice, so my advice is to consult your vet.

DIARRHOEA
Overfeeding, a sudden change of diet or a chill can cause upset tummies, especially in puppies.

Stop all food for 24 hours, but make sure your Bulldog has access to fresh water – never milk. Restart feeding with small amounts of plain, boiled rice with chicken or fish. After a couple of days, gradually reintroduce the normal diet, but if the problem persists, consult your vet.

EXTERNAL PARASITES

FLEAS
Being a short-coated breed, it is

usually quite easy to see if a Bulldog has fleas. The first sign is continuous scratching, and, on close inspection, you will find flea droppings, which look like small specks or grains of sand in the coat. Usually, the fleas will be found around the tail area or on the head and neck. They are most prevalent in the summer and the quickest cure is to bathe your dog in a good insecticidal shampoo, towel him and put him out in the sun to dry off completely. There are also various flea sprays on the market. If you find your Bulldog prone to picking up fleas, use one of the preventative methods throughout the summer. You can also purchase special treatments for your carpets and furniture.

Bulldogs are sensitive to the heat, and should never be exposed to the sun for prolonged periods.

If in doubt, your vet should be happy to give you advice on a suitable flea programme.

TICKS

Ticks are much less common than fleas and are normally only picked up from the grass in a field where sheep have been. They are small, round, bloodsucking insects that bury their heads into the dog's skin and swell into a reddish-brown pea-sized blob, similar to a wart. Care must be taken in removing them, as the head must not be left in the skin. Soak a swab with surgical spirit or ether, and apply to the tick. This will loosen it, and it can then be removed intact.

EYES

CHERRY EYE

The common term for the prolapse of a gland behind the third eyelid, Cherry Eye occasionally occurs in young puppies, usually around the age of 10-16 weeks. A small, pink, pea-like lump appears in the inner corner of the eye. This can be gently pushed back into place, but invariably it will prolapse

again and require surgery. New owners are understandably worried, as it does look uncomfortable, but it is a minor operation. Some vets will even remove the gland under local anaesthetic, and the puppy recovers completely within hours.

ENTROPION

This is a condition which occurs when the eyelids turn in and the lashes irritate the eye, causing considerable discomfort. You will find that your dog has a continuous nasty discharge from the eye, which is almost impossible to cure with eye drops or creams, and usually requires surgery. Dogs or bitches with this condition should never be bred from.

FEET

Cysts on feet can be a problem. A lesion appears between the toes and makes it painful for the dog to walk. To treat it, dissolve a dessertspoonful of sea salt in warm water in a small bucket, and stand the affected foot in the water for a few minutes. This will help to disperse the swelling. If your Bulldog is continually licking his feet, examine the pads – you may find he has a small wound that needs treating, or even a tiny stone stuck in his pad.

HEATSTROKE

All short-nosed breeds (like Pugs, Pekingese, etc. – also known as 'brachycephalic') must be carefully managed in very hot weather. Bulldogs will often lie in the full sun with no ill effects, but they should be left quietly, on their own, with plenty of shade to move into when required. Never walk your Bulldog in the heat of the day, or allow children to run and chase him around the garden – he must be left to decide for himself where he wants to be. During the summer months, I always exercise my dogs early in the morning and later in the evening.

Never leave your dog in the conservatory when you go out. I recently heard about two Bulldogs who were left in a conservatory at eight o'clock on a cold frosty morning. By the time the owner returned home for lunch, the sun had come out, the temperature had soared, and both dogs tragically died.

Never leave your dog in the car unattended. Even with a window open, the car temperature will rapidly rise, and, within minutes, it could be fatal. Being a short-faced breed, the Bulldog finds it more difficult to cope with humid conditions. There have been many tragic cases, most of which could have been avoided if more care had been taken.

Travelling can be a problem in very hot weather, and it can be very worrying if you are held up in traffic in the heat. Always be prepared with a large container of water, towels, and, if possible, ice. Save your old plastic lemonade bottles, fill them with water and put them in the freezer overnight. You will find they make excellent coolers to put inside your dog's cage in the car. If you use a crate in your car, make sure it is the wire type so that plenty of air can circulate. Soak a towel in icy water and let him lie on it. There are also special ice-pack collars now on the market, which can be useful to keep the dog's temperature down while travelling.

The first signs of heatstroke in your Bulldog are: extremely rapid, heavy panting, and his tongue may go blue as he gasps for air. This will progress into 'roaring' – a term we use to describe when he is really in distress and struggling to breathe. At this stage, he may vomit a white froth, which you must clear from his throat with your fingers. Use a hosepipe to cool him down and spray him all over, particularly on the neck and tail areas, or submerse him up to the neck in deep water. Do not allow him to drink too much, as this will make him sick or cause him to choke on the froth

produced. He must be kept quiet until his normal breathing pattern returns; this can take up to half an hour.

KENNEL COUGH

As the name suggests, kennel cough is more commonly found in large kennels. It is extremely infectious and spreads rapidly. Your dog will cough harshly, sounding as if he has a bone stuck in his throat, and he may vomit a white froth. It is not usually life-threatening to healthy dogs, and once they have been infected, they usually gain immunity. However, it can be serious in young puppies and elderly dogs. If you suspect your Bulldog may have kennel cough, consult your vet and do not allow the dog to mix with other dogs for a period of three weeks. If you intend to leave him in boarding kennels at any time, he must be vaccinated against parainfluenza.

PYOMETRA

Pyometra occasionally occurs, usually in older bitches, one to two months after a season. The

uterus fills with pus and you will see a thick red-brown evil-smelling discharge from the vulva. You will notice the bitch drinking excessively, and she will have a high temperature. If you suspect this condition, seek veterinary advice immediately.

SKIN CONDITIONS

Wet eczema is the most common skin complaint with Bulldogs, but it is not contagious, so you do not have to worry about isolation. It can erupt very quickly and spread from a small spot into a huge patch within hours. It can be caused by the dog scratching an itchy flea bite, stress, or even an excessively rich diet, and is usually worse in the hot months. The first sign is continuous scratching, often on the neck or shoulder. Check the skin for any red patches or lesions; the quicker it is treated, the more likely you are to control it. Tea tree oil or aloe vera are cheap, successful cures if sprayed on as soon as the first symptoms appear. If left unattended, wet eczema can be difficult to cure quickly and may need veterinary treatment. Antihistamine tablets can also help to stop the irritation.

TAIL
Bulldog tails vary from medium-length and straight (as mentioned in the Standard) to short, screw tails, but they are never docked.

The very tight screw tail can be a problem in the hot weather, when the area becomes moist and causes irritation. Bathe the affected parts with a little mild disinfectant in water, dry thoroughly, and apply a little medicated powder. If the problem persists, your Bulldog may need veterinary treatment. In severe cases, it may mean having the tail removed, but this is very rare.

GIVING MEDICATION
It is not difficult to give tablets to Bulldogs. Being a greedy breed, they will happily eat most things. Disguise the pill in a knob of butter, cheese or meat and it will

Ch. Outdoors Country Gent enjoying excellent health at eight years of age.

be swallowed before he realises. Liquid medicine is more difficult, and I find the easiest way is to use a syringe (minus the needle). Lift his top lip and put the syringe into the side of his jaw and quickly empty. Hold the mouth shut and rub his throat until he swallows.

If your puppy has been prescribed antibiotics, it can be advantageous to feed live natural yoghurt. This helps to restore the beneficial flora bacteria in the digestive system, as these can be destroyed when antibiotics are given. Give one teaspoonful twice a day after the course is completed, because antibiotics will destroy the good bacteria in the yoghurt.

CARE OF THE VETERAN

We all have to face the fact that our beloved pet will not live forever. All dogs age differently – some have really slowed down by the age of eight, while others are still active at ten. I find that the older they get, the more their characters show.

A Bulldog will never complain, so you must feel for him. When he has been your constant companion for many years, you will sense when he is failing. His eyesight and hearing may deteriorate, and his joints stiffen up.

Make sure he is warm at night, feed him two small meals a day instead of one, and, if he has lost his teeth, you may need to moisten his biscuit.

Try not to let him become overweight, and make sure he drinks enough. Check his toenails – if he is taking less exercise, they may need cutting.

Everyone hopes their pets will pass away peacefully in their sleep, but this is not always to be. You will know when it is only your

Bulldog's great courage keeping him going – do not let him suffer.

However difficult it may seem, do not keep him alive for your sake – be fair to him and allow him a dignified end in repayment for all the pleasure he has given you. No dog should endure weeks of pain when there is no hope of recovery.

Talk to your vet and ask for a home visit. The vet can then examine the dog, and, if it is necessary, put him to rest in the surroundings he knows and loves, while you comfort him. He will gently slip away and be free from pain. This is your final kindness to your best friend.